accidental

THE AIRBNB HOST

YOUR ROOM-BY-ROOM EXPERT
GUIDE TO A 5-STAR GUEST STAY

accidental

THE AIRBNB HOST

YOUR ROOM-BY-ROOM EXPERT GUIDE TO A 5-STAR GUEST STAY

VERONICA TERCAN

Written by Veronica Tercan
Cover and interior design by Carolyn Brown
Cover and interior illustrations by Latorri Lindsay
Edited by Jessica Vozel

ISBN: 978-0-9981293-1-0 (Black & White edition)
ISBN: 978-0-9981293-0-3 (Colored edition)

First edition, November 2016

"A merry host makes merry guests"

DUTCH PROVERB

Contents

RESOURCES FOR ACCIDENTAL HOSTS

FOREWORD

It was the beginning of 2014, and Airbnb was booming in the Bay Area.

Having left behind its identity as a niche offering for free-spirited travelers, Airbnb seemed to be taking over the world. Or at least our part of it.

Countless people and startups in San Francisco were looking to ride the wave of Airbnb's success, and everyone you met in the Bay Area had a story about staying in, or renting out, an Airbnb property. Myself included!

After hosting for a few years in my own San Francisco apartment, in 2014 I decided to join Urban Bellhop, a startup for Airbnb management that offered host services like booking, cleaning, and marketing.

Working with Urban Bellhop, I started to fully understand what was happening.

INTRODUCING THE "ACCIDENTAL HOST"

We were (and still are) in the midst of a huge shift in the hospitality industry...and in the way we think about travel, tourism, and vacation. Gone are the days of faceless hotel rooms filled with strangers, and in its place are authentic accommodations and new friends meeting all over the world.

And, at the same time, people are jumping into this new hospitality landscape feet first. So many that there's a name for them: "Accidental Airbnb Hosts."

What do I mean by "Accidental Host"?

Because the barrier to entry is low, most people (myself included, again!) turn into Airbnb hosts seemingly overnight. Even if we think about it for months beforehand, as soon as we click the button to create our Airbnb listing, we have just jumped right into the water...almost as if by accident.

NOW WE HAVE TO SWIM

In order to stay afloat, we become very well-versed very quickly in the *logistics* of Airbnb. How to handle bookings and taxes. How much to charge per night. How to effectively market our properties. How to keep our property and belongings safe. Understandably, our primary concern is getting guests in the door, making a profit, and safeguarding ourselves from potential problems.

In the process, though, we sometimes miss the very thing that set Airbnb apart: the **exceptional guest experience**. The stuff between "booking" and "goodbye." After all, happy guests are the key to making this whole thing *work*. Happy guests mean 5-star reviews, referrals, and the satisfaction of helping strangers get to know and love the place that *you* love.

WHY I WROTE THIS BOOK

It's normal that we don't know all the shiny hotel tips and tricks for hospitality; it's still a new industry to us (and they award entire college degrees in this stuff)! But it all works out when we learn from our mistakes and make improvements along the way.

Which is why I wrote this book. I wanted to teach other "accidental hosts" (and those who have been hosting for a while but could use a tune-up) **how to become overnight hospitality experts and provide a 5-star guest stay.** Every time.

To do this, I gathered tips from long-time Airbnb and hospitality industry experts...and I learned a *lot*. From decorating techniques that create an inspiring, must-book-now vacation rental, to where to find high-quality wrinkle free bedding, to cleaning tips that every Airbnb host *must* know. And I even discovered my favorite bath mat in the world.

(Believe me, when it comes to managing your Airbnb rental as efficiently as a hotel, it's all in the details.

You want to meet my bath mat and my wrinkle free sheets!)

THIS BOOK CONSISTS OF TWO PARTS.

In **Part One** (chapters 1-5) we'll talk about getting started. I'll cover the importance of **creating trust** using your profile picture and description, how to **optimize** your listing to get more bookings and rank high in the Airbnb search, and how to **screen your guests** and prepare them for arrival. Then I'll end with my definitive list of **cleaning hacks** for Airbnb hosts.

In **Part Two** (chapters 6-10) we get down to the details. I'll take you room by room through your rental and teach you how to make that room exceptional. From the perfect guestroom, to bathroom essentials and must-have kitchen items, to decorating tips that put guest comfort first. And, most importantly, I'll talk how to **make sure your guests rave about your property** and come back again and again.

The best part? The last page of every chapter includes a handy, one-page checklist with a bite-sized breakdown of what you need to know from that chapter. So, if you're short on time, you can skim these checklists, keep them in your back pocket, and get a great overview of what you'll need to do to go from "accidental host" to "kick-ass host."

Whether you're just getting started with Airbnb, or looking for ways to improve your hospitality skills and increase your Airbnb success, you can get started today with this book.

Thanks for reading!

Veronica Tercan

Part

01

GETTING STARTED

USER PROFILE

TRUST IS EARNED, NOT GIVEN

WANT TO KNOW THE #1 most important thing you can do, *today*, to get more bookings?

Put some time and care into crafting an excellent user profile.

As a host, you know how happy you feel when you click on a potential guest's profile and realize she or he seems warm, friendly, and genuinely enthusiastic about visiting. (If you haven't experienced that feeling yet--you will!) In other words, you feel like you can trust the guest...and it's a huge relief.

Create that same feeling for *guests* with a profile that lets them know they can trust you, too. After all, in a sometimes untrustworthy world full of skeptics, proving that people actually *can* be good is one of the most important things an Airbnb host can do. Show that you're one of the good ones, and you'll be rewarded in bookings!

So, how do you show trustworthiness with a few words and a picture? Follow the checklist steps below!

1. UPLOAD YOUR BEST PROFILE PICTURE.

Recent research[1] from The Ohio State University shows that, more than any other element on our social media pages, our profile photos impact the way others perceive us.

Your Airbnb profile is no different. Many potential guests will check out your profile photo first, searching for clues about your trustworthiness (that word again), approachability and overall attitude. Will they be comfortable sharing a space with you? Or, at the very least, giving you a chunk of their hard-earned cash?

Make no mistake: you don't have have to be model-gorgeous to rent your property! However, the photo should be one *you* feel good about, and one that captures who you really are. A genuine smile works wonders! **Avoid wearing sunglasses or hats** that hide your face and make it difficult for people to get a read on you.

To get your best side, and ensure your photo is top-

1   Van Der Heide, Brandon, Jonathan D. D'Angelo and Erin M. Schumaker. "The Effects of Verbal Versus Photographic Self-Presentation on Impression Formation." Journal of Communication. 62.1 (2012): 98-116.

quality and not grainy or sketchy-looking, **consider hiring a professional photographer**. Bonus: you can use the pro photo on your other social media profiles, too!

2. BUILD TRUST WITH YOUR BIO.

After checking out your photo and making a snap judgement, potential guests are going to read your bio to determine if they've judged you correctly. Make it count!

When you fill in your bio, **put yourself in your guests' shoes**. What would you want to know about your host if you were looking for a place to stay? Tell them where you're from, where you live now, why you love your surrounding city, town or neighborhood, and what you do for a living (and for fun).

Most importantly, now that you're part of the Airbnb community, tell them why you decided to join. Of course, the obvious reason is to make extra money, but dig deeper. Many of your guests won't want to think of their Airbnb stay as just another business transaction.

Instead, consider the non-monetary benefits, like making new connections with people from all corners of the globe. After all, having the opportunity to welcome the whole world into your living room *is* pretty remarkable, right? Share that enthusiasm in your profile!

3. EARN A VERIFIED ID BADGE.

Don't skip this next trust-building step.

Airbnb created **identity verification** to match your

online identity with your real-world identity. When they match, you get a badge similar to Twitter's "verified account" checkmark. This, of course, puts guests' minds at ease and proves you're not a con artist or a middle-aged man posing as a twenty-something woman.

To verify your identity with Airbnb, you will need to upload a profile photo and a photo of your passport or driver's license, provide your email address, and connect to your Facebook, Google or LinkedIn account. Don't worry--the information you provide to Airbnb is sent using SSL, which privately and securely transmits sensitive information such as credit card numbers and IDs.

4. WORK ON YOUR 5-STAR REVIEWS.

If your photos create the great first impression, your bio solidifies that impression, and your verified ID badge proves that you are *you*, your reviews lay to rest any lingering worries. We trust the opinions of others. That's why, more than any other element on your user profile, your reviews can really tip the scales toward a new booking or a "no, thanks."

If you're new to Airbnb and don't have reviews yet, don't worry. You can invite a few friends to write a *recommendation* of you instead, focusing on the parts of your personality that make you excellent at hosting guests. Maybe it's your fun-loving nature, your generosity, your knowledge of the city, or your careful attention to all the little details in your home.

By reading positive (and truthful!) things others have

written about you, your first guests will see that your profile is honest. In the meantime, you can work on getting that first 5-star review!

5. COMPLETE THE "ABOUT ME" SECTION.

On your profile page, you will see an extra space where you can add more information about where you work, the schools you attended, and the languages you speak. It may seem like unimportant information, but actually, it's an excellent opportunity to connect with guests who have something in common with you.

If you and your potential guest went to the same school, for example, Airbnb may display your listing more prominently to him or her. Imagine all the amazing conversations that might follow with someone who went to your high school or college! (*"Remember that teacher we used to call 'Snowman' because of dandruff on his jacket?"*) Or maybe your guests notice that you work at a company they really love. You can probably guess what happens next. They not only want to stay at your place, but they want to meet *you*, as well!

6. BECOME A SUPERHOST.

Another way to convince your guests they're in good hands is to become a **Superhost.** While the "Superhost" status doesn't improve your property's search ranking, it does come with a few perks. First, you'll get a Superhost badge on your profile, which is a convenient shorthand that tells guests "this host is high-quality and worth a closer look!"

Plus, Superhosts who maintain their status for a full year receive a $100 travel coupon, in addition to priority Airbnb phone support and product previews.

So, how do you become a Superhost? Pay attention to these four metrics:

- **Hosting Experience**: You have hosted at least 10 completed trips.
- **Reviews:** At least 80% of the reviews you receive are 5 stars.
- **Response Rate:** You respond to inquiries and reservation requests within 24 hours at least 90% of the time.
- **Commitment:** You avoid canceling confirmed reservations.

Monitor your hosting performance on your dashboard to see how you're doing in these four key areas!

If you've completed these six steps, and created a well-rounded, honest and engaging user profile, congratulations! You're well on your way to being the person your guests want to entrust with their upcoming trip.

On Airbnb, building a solid relationship with your guests before meeting in person can have a huge impact in your booking rate. Unlike a chain hotel or a billion-dollar resort, you're not only selling a place to stay, you're selling the guest's potential experience with you.

Of course, that's not to say the "place to stay" part is unimportant! Your next goal is to create an Airbnb listing about your property that matches your sparkling host personality and creates an impression of your space that guests can't resist. More on that in the next chapter!

AIRBNB CHECKLIST 01

6 STEPS TO CREATING A STELLAR PROFILE

1. UPLOAD YOUR BEST PROFILE PICTURE
A smiling, high-quality profile photo
will create a winning first impression.

☐

2. BUILD TRUST WITH YOUR BIO
An honest bio makes you a real person
to your guests. Tell them what you're
all about!

☐

3. EARN A VERIFIED ID BADGE
A complete profile, photo of your ID,
and valid e-mail/social media links
award you a badge.

☐

4. WORK ON YOUR 5-STAR REVIEWS
Short on reviews? Invite a few friends
to leave a glowing reference.

☐

5. COMPLETE THE "ABOUT ME" SECTION
Add where you live, your alma mater,
and the languages you speak. These
can be a convo starter!

☐

6. BECOME A SUPERHOST
Show your guests they're in good
hands by earning your Superhost badge.

☐

LISTING

HOOK GUESTS WITH A STELLAR LISTING

While working as a vacation rental manager in Los Angeles, I was able to see and appreciate so many beautiful homes and neighborhoods.

One of my all-time favorite places, though, was a modern downtown Los Angeles loft. High ceilings, exposed piping in the living room, large windows, polished concrete floors...this rental was just stunning inside. Outside, the building had an idyllic urban courtyard, where people could chat with their neighbours, walk their dogs, or grab a bite to eat.

If I didn't love the place enough already, I also discovered a tiny sushi place tucked away on a street close to the building courtyard. After a few months of bringing my client's guests here to introduce them to the neighborhood, and ordering the same dish again and again, the kind owners nicknamed me Eelmonster (after my favorite sushi). Needless to say, I truly loved visiting this beautiful apartment and neighborhood. The whole place was like an oasis in the middle of the busy DTLA Fashion District.

But there was a problem. You couldn't tell any of this when you looked at my client's listing!

The photos were dark and unwelcoming. The description of his loft was dry... basically just a short summary of amenities. It broke my heart to think that people were passing up on this gem I loved so much! So, we decided to make improvements. We requested a photographer on Airbnb, wrote a more appealing description, and started experimenting with ways to increase his search ranking on Airbnb and Google.

The photos *alone* made a huge difference. Not only did guests start showering the loft with compliments in their inquiries, there was a marked increase in bookings, as well.

In this chapter I'll give you tips on how to be the next Airbnb success story and create a listing that attracts your ideal guest. And I'll also share my crack-the-code secrets for two much-discussed topics: how to rank higher on Airbnb, and how to use social media to drive more traffic to your listing!

1. UPLOAD GREAT PHOTOS.

Just as with your profile photo, the photos you upload to

showcase your rental will influence your potential guest's all-important first impression.

I dare say that photos are even more important than your written description. If your guests aren't hypnotized by the gorgeous photos of your rental, they won't click on your listing. And if they don't click, they won't even *see* the description. Let your photos speak for you in those short, precious seconds your guests are scanning their Airbnb search results.

You guessed it: you should **seriously consider hiring a professional photographer**. It's never been easier (or cheaper): Airbnb allows you to request a photographer through them *for free*. Or, if you'd rather have more control of the process, ask around, read reviews, check out portfolios, and find the best photographer you can afford.

It's also important to **choose your most beautiful picture as your main photo**, because it'll show up in the search results. If your rental house (or treehouse, or Airstream trailer, or igloo) has great curb appeal, choose an exterior photo as your main shot. If your rental is part of a condo unit or apartment building, use a well-lit shot of your most striking interior room.

Be sure to **upload photos of every room of your house**, as well, and also include photos of outdoor areas, plus a few of your neighborhood.

2. WRITE AN APPEALING DESCRIPTION.

So, your potential guest has clicked on your gorgeous photos and is now reading your description. Great. Here is where you give them a bunch of good reasons to choose your place over your competition!

Avoid writing a bland list of features with no personality. Instead, write down *benefits*--what people can do in your house and neighborhood. If you have a terrace with a gorgeous view, describe that view. If you live next to a delicious bakery, point out that they can have fresh-baked bread and coffee when they roll out of bed.

Paint a picture of what guests will see, feel, hear, and even taste when they stay at your sanctuary.

DON'T KNOW WHERE TO START? HERE ARE SOME HELPFUL TIPS.

1. **Take a look at other listings in your area.** Scope out the competition. What do you have in your rental that they don't? Maybe you have a nice garden where guests can drink their morning coffee. Or maybe they'll wake up to the sound of ocean waves. Or maybe you live on a vibrant street filled with the coolest bars in the city. These are your **unique selling points** and they should be mentioned early and often!

2. **Think about the history of your rental**. In other words, its *story*. For example, I'm writing this book from the former "Facebook Mansion," where Mark Zuckerberg and other Facebook founders lived for a time while building their empire. Its new life is as a community for startup founders and tech innovators to live and work together, all drawn to the story of this historic Silicon Valley house. Think about your rental in a similar way. What was the space like before you got there? Even

consider your own **personal connection** to the place... your own story. What drew *you* to it in the first place? Likely those same things will draw your potential guests, too, so share them!

3. If you have existing reviews from past guests, **take note of anything they mention as their favorite features in your rental**. If you don't have any reviews yet, go ahead and check out the reviews of other Airbnb properties. If you share common features that *their* guests rave about, go ahead and include them in your own listing. As long as it's true, and you don't steal the review word-for-word, it's not cheating!

When you're done, have someone you trust **proofread** your listing. Nothing cuts into your professional impression (and the readability of your listing) like a bunch of spelling and grammar errors!

Or, if you hate writing, you can always hire a professional travel copywriter to do it for you. They know what travelers are looking for, and how to prove to them that you're the obvious choice. Rates per description vary between $50 and $200, depending on the writer's background and experience...and it's definitely worth every penny!

3. SET A COMPETITIVE PRICE.

Now for a challenge: you have to figure out what to charge!

When setting your nightly price, Airbnb will offer a suggested rate on that same page. Before taking their suggestion, check out some similar listings in your area to get a sense of their pricing first. That way, you can find your "sweet spot" based on Airbnb's recommendation *and* what your competition is charging.

When you're just starting out, it's worth offering a lower rate than your competition until you build a solid base of positive reviews. After that point, the key will be to offer a better and better rental experience as your nightly rate increases. Remember: travelers are looking for a good deal *and* a top-notch trip. And some of the most popular Airbnb listings...the ones with hundreds of 5-star reviews... are the ones that deliver a 5-star guest stay combined with a reasonable rate, usually around $100 per night. (Stay tuned to Part 2 of this book, which teaches you exactly how to create that 5-star stay!)

Keep in mind that there will *always* be guests who ask for a discount. You may have good reason to give them one. But be sure to set limits. Though it's tempting to dip well below your target nightly rate to land a booking, you should know what your place is worth, and what you need to net to make your desired profit... and stick to it!

4. DEFINE YOUR IDEAL GUESTS.

To craft an even better listing, you should determine who your ideal guest is and what benefits your home will provide for *them*, specifically. In other words, think like a marketer. Before crafting a campaign message to promote a product, marketers think about the product's benefits and their ideal customer first and foremost. Then, they speak right in their ear.

Follow these two steps to define your ideal guest:

STEP 1:

Write out a list of each feature of your place and the benefits they provide. Here are a few features of the Facebook Mansion and the benefits for guests, for example:

- The Facebook Mansion provides a one-of-a-kind experience in the birthplace of the biggest social network in the world.
- Co-working areas allow guests to work on their own projects while socializing with other entrepreneurs in the house.
- Its excellent location is close to Silicon Valley biggest technology companies.
- Residents from different backgrounds come together here. Making new friends is practically a given!
- Everyone gets a private room with a queen bed to relax after a busy day.

STEP 2:

Using that list of features you brainstormed, determine the type of guest who would love to stay at your place. The ideal guest for the Facebook Mansion, of course, is a tech entrepreneur interested in making new connections with like-minded people. For your rental, it might be families, couples, business travelers, pet-lovers...Those are the people to whom your listing should be directed. Put yourself in their shoes!

5. BE CLEAR ABOUT HOUSE RULES.

It's also important to **set guest expectations and rules in your listing** to help guests decide if you're a good fit. Some hosts don't have house rules and rely on common sense, but in my experience, you need to be clear about whether pets or smoking is allowed, what time they can check in, etc. Your guests will appreciate these clear rules, too. That way they know exactly how to move around in your house and make it their own without feeling uncomfortable.

If you live in an apartment building, **be clear about specific building rules** to avoid problems with your neighbors. Also be honest about any factors that could potentially bother your guests, like a noisy neighborhood. I used to live (and host Airbnb guests) very close to a fire station in downtown San Francisco. The firetrucks woke me up every single night. I loved living in this magical city, so I didn't mind that much. But my guests deserved to be warned!

Maybe I lost a booking or two by mentioning the sirens outright on my listing, but it likely saved me from some scathing reviews, which would have been far more damaging in the long run.

6. BOOST YOUR RANKING.

Unfortunately, there is no magic bullet to becoming a top-ranked property. It takes work and time. But take heart: there are a few things you can do right off the bat.

First, be sure to fill out every section of your listing in detail. Your listing's placement in the Airbnb search results depends, in part, on how closely a guest's specific search matches your listing. So, the more detailed you are, the wider the net you cast.

Airbnb also rewards hosts that deliver a great experience to guests (and thus get great reviews). In short, the better you are as a host, and the better your reviews, the higher your listing will rank. This is good news, of course...it means you can take control of your own success! Take a look at the list below for more tips on how to boost your listing's placement on Airbnb.

HOW TO BOOST YOUR AIRBNB RANKING

IMPROVE YOUR LISTING
Professional photos and a clear, accurate description may raise your listing's search placement.

SET A COMPETITIVE PRICE
Check the market in your area and price competitively, especially if you're just starting out.

COLLECT GREAT REVIEWS
Follow the rules in this book for 5-star stays! Both the quantity *and* quality of guest reviews make a difference.

ALLOW INSTANT BOOK
Airbnb favors Instant Book; enable it and watch your rental ranking get a big boost.

RESPOND WITHIN 24 HOURS
Get good at communicating with potential guests! Expired reservation requests will count against you.

DON'T CANCEL RESERVATIONS
Save cancellations for *true* emergencies, because voided reservations hurt your search placement.

VERIFY YOUR ID
Let travelers know you are who you say you are by verifying your ID and connecting your social accounts.

LINK TO FACEBOOK
Don't forget Facebook! If you have friends in common with the traveler, your listing may display more prominently.

7. RISE UP GOOGLE'S RANKS.

All of the above factors help to boost your rankings within Airbnb's own website or app. But if you want even more visibility for your listing, your next goal is to get on the first pages of *Google*. To accomplish this, you must first focus on overall **quality of your listing and rental.** All the tricks in the world won't help if your property isn't among the best!

Head over to Google and search for an Airbnb rental in, say, downtown Milan, Italy. If you type "Milan" "downtown" and "Airbnb" you'll see that gorgeous, high-quality, professionally decorated and photographed rentals dominate the first page of Google results. Take a page from their playbook! You can also optimize your title and listing description with relevant keywords (like "Milan" and "downtown" in the example above) to boost your ranking.

From there, the results will snowball: the more people click on your awesome listing, the higher your placement will be in the search results. And the higher you are in the search results, the more clicks you'll get! This applies to both Google *and* Airbnb's internal search.

If you only want to be seen on Airbnb and *not* in search engines like Google (if you're concerned about privacy, for example) you can turn off search indexing in your privacy settings in your account.

8. PROMOTE YOUR LISTING ON SOCIAL MEDIA.

Done with #7? Now it's time to move on to promoting your rental on **social media.** Simply put: social media drives traffic, and traffic bumps your listing up in search results. And that means more bookings.

Here's a how-to breakdown, with tips for using some of the most popular social media platforms to boost your Google ranking.

INSTAGRAM

The rise of visual-based social media platforms like Pinterest and Instagram has been great for the travel industry. After all, our travels are often the most photographed moments of our lives. And what photographs better than a beautiful place?

Take advantage!

On Instagram, you can only post photos via smartphone app. Be choosy with filters; contrary to popular belief, they don't always enhance your photos! Add an attractive description and **include keywords**, like your location or fun things about your rental, as well as relevant **hashtags** so people who search those hashtags can find your photo.

If your place is in Milan, for example, you can use hashtags like #Milan, #Milano, #Italy #vacation #airbnb #travel, etc., to target Instagram users who are thinking about a trip to Milan and want to explore a little bit on social media first. Don't forget to tag Airbnb in your photo by typing @Airbnb. And it's an easy step that could pay off: Airbnb often selects rental photos to post on their Instagram account. Instant traffic!

Keep in mind that Instragram photo's aren't "clickable," which means you can't link to your property. And the only place where you can add a URL is in your bio. The goal here is to create brand awareness, so they can seek out your rental on Airbnb's website.

Another savvy way to bump up visibility for your rental, *and* create a sense of community with your guests on Instagram? Ask them to share favorite moments from their stay and recommendations for future guests using a **unique hashtag** you created. Think of it as an interactive, digital version of a traditional guestbook.

This way, prospective and current guests can search your hashtag and see the photos posted by previous guests. A lot of people will share photos of their vacation on Instagram *anyway*, and it takes very little effort to just go ahead include your hashtag in their post, as a virtual "thank you" to their host--you! You can even **add your Instagram hashtag to your Airbnb listing description** so potential guests can explore and see more photos of your place.

Big brands use Instagram in this same way, and slap a fancy marketing name on it: User Generated Content (UGC). UCG creates engagement, expands a brand's reach, brings together a community and fosters brand loyalty.

Who says you can't do the same thing for your rental?

PINTEREST

Pinterest is one of the fastest growing social networks and one of the largest drivers of website traffic.[1] And good news: the travel industry is perfectly suited to Pinterest, too, as people often create dream boards to inspire their travels. In contrast to Instagram, you can make images on Pinterest "clickable" by including a link to your Airbnb listing.

Create different boards related to your Airbnb listing, and categorize your photos so they appear in search results. For instance, if you have a bohemian home in Barcelona, you can make boards with the titles "Barcelona" or "Things to do in Barcelona" or "Bohemian Homes." It doesn't hurt to include the same images of your rental across several boards...just be sure the boards *also* have other interesting and beautiful images.

Add an attractive description to the photos and use several appropriate hashtags to expand the reach of your images. You can directly upload images to Pinterest (don't forget to include the link!) or you can use the "Pin It"

1   Mander, Jason. "Pinterest was the fastest growing social network in 2014." Global Web Index. 21 January 2015.

button to quickly pin content found anywhere online to your personal Pinterest account.

Importantly, always make sure your pins link back to *your* Airbnb listing, not just the Airbnb website!

FACEBOOK

I can't finish this section without mentioning that Goliath of social media: Facebook. When it comes to social media traffic, recent research shows that Facebook drives **four times** more traffic than Pinterest and **three times** more than the other six social networks - Twitter, StumbleUpon, Reddit, Google+, YouTube and LinkedIn - *combined.*[2]

You may be thinking "haven't people gotten bored of Facebook?" Maybe. But for now, it still boasts over 1 billion users--bored or not! And when it comes to targeting a very specific audience, Facebook is king. Whether you share the link to your Airbnb listing on your personal Facebook profile, or create a professional Facebook page for your Airbnb listing, you will drive traffic and create awareness among your friends (and beyond!).

You may have noticed you can connect your Facebook account to your Airbnb account. It can pay off! With this feature, Airbnb uses Facebook data to show if you and travelers have shared friends, and your listing may display more prominently to travelers with whom you have friends in common. And, at the same time, the traveler

2   Wong, Danny. "Report: Facebook Drives 4x More Traffic than Pinterest." The Shareaholic Blog. 27 October 2014.

might feel safer (and more likely to book!) knowing you have a mutual connection.

Visit the "Trust and Verification" section located in your Airbnb profile to connect your Airbnb and Facebook accounts.

AIRBNB CHECKLIST 02

7 STEPS TO CREATING
A STELLAR LISTING

1. UPLOAD GREAT PHOTOS
Quality photos boost bookings more
than any other tool. Consider investing
in a professional! ☐

2. WRITE AN APPEALING DESCRIPTION
Avoid bland lists of features. Detail
what guests will see, feel, hear and
taste when they stay. ☐

3. SET A COMPETITIVE PRICE
Offer a lower-than-average rate to
gather guests and good reviews...then
raise it as you climb. ☐

4. DEFINE YOUR IDEAL GUEST
A solid guest/host match prevents
misunderstandings and increases
guest satisfaction. ☐

5. BE CLEAR ABOUT HOUSE RULES
Clear rules, conveyed in a friendly tone,
will help guests decide if your home is
a good fit. ☐

6. BOOST YOUR RANKING
Airbnb rewards hosts that deliver great
experiences. The better your reviews,
the higher you rank! ☐

7. PROMOTE YOUR LISTING
Use keywords in your title and
description and share your listing
on social media. ☐

PRE-BOOKING

YOU HAD ME AT "HELLO"

A SUCCESSFUL HOSTING EXPERIENCE BEGINS long before you welcome guests. In fact, it starts the moment you receive the reservation request. And, make no mistake, it's not just about how *you* handle those first interactions.

Of course, you should be concerned about making a strong and welcoming impression. But don't forget that you will be bringing strangers into your home! Before accepting a reservation, you need to do a little research to find out if *they're* trustworthy, too. Thankfully, Airbnb has built multiple features to help you screen guests, including a messaging system, user reviews and Verified ID. Make use of these features and safeguard yourself (and your property).

And check out the recommended steps below for ensuring your hosting experience is stress-free from the get-go!

1. CHECK GUESTS' PROFILES.

When a reservation request comes in, don't be lured by the excitement of a potential booking. Think like an online dater and check their picture and profile first! It's the best way to get a good first impression. And, as with online dating, beware of sparse info or a barely filled-out profile...it could be a warning sign. But it's not *always* a dealbreaker. If potential guests have incomplete profiles, give them another chance and ask them to upload a picture of themselves and complete the Verified ID process. Maybe they're a first-time Airbnb user and just need a little bit of guidance!

To further safeguard, you can also require your guests to have a Verified ID in order to submit a reservation request in the first place. On your dashboard, go to "Your Listings" and click on "Reservation Requirements." Then, check the box that reads: "Require guests to go through verification."

2. CHECK REVIEWS & REFERENCES.

Next, check out your potential guest's reviews from Airbnb hosts he or she has stayed with in the past. Just as your reviews are like gold to potential guests, reviews of guests are gold for *you*. If they've been negatively reviewed, feel free to use the messaging system to ask as many questions as you want.

If, at the end of that conversation you decide you don't want to accept a guest inquiry, make sure to **officially** 'decline' the request. Simply sending a message, or not responding at all, can negatively affect your rating on the site.

3. ASK TARGETED QUESTIONS.

If guests don't have reviews or references, use the messaging system to learn more about them. Messaging guests with the right questions before a booking lets you know if they're a good fit. My favorite question is: "Why are you visiting us here in [destination]?" It's a great conversation starter, *and* it helps you accommodate any special needs they may have related to their trip...that's the stuff great hosts are made of!

4. CONSULT SOCIAL MEDIA.

If you're still hesitant about accepting a guest, search his or her social media profiles. Most people have an online profile on Twitter, Facebook, Instagram or LinkedIn these days. Some even have a personal website or blog. In this case, the dating rule of "don't Google before a first date" does not apply! "Stalk" away; it's for your own good!

Compare guests' social profiles to their Airbnb profiles and make sure the details line up. If you can't find them on social networks, see if they mention where they work on the "About" section of their Airbnb profile. If they do, Google his or her name together with the company name and check for hits. If you still have no luck, ask questions in the messaging system until you feel comfortable accepting the guest.

Note: Airbnb hides websites and phone numbers in their messaging system prior to reservations, but they won't hide names and company names. So go ahead and ask for their workplace!

5. RESPOND QUICKLY TO INQUIRIES.

Now that you've done some background investigation, it's time to prove yourself to your guests! First, respond as fast as you can to any reservation requests. Most guests send inquiries to several hosts at the same time...and usually book with the host from whom they received the fastest response. Responding quickly shows that you'll be fast to respond to any issues that may arise during their trip, too.

6. USE THEIR FIRST NAME.

"A person's name is to that person the sweetest and most important sound in any language," writes Dale Carnegie, author of the iconic book *How to Win Friends and Influence People.*

When replying to guest inquiries in messages, always use your guest's first name. A name is a core part of our identity, and hearing it makes us feel special and respected. For your part, remembering someone's name, and using it, is a great way to stand out from the impersonal inquiry responses your guest is surely getting from other hosts.

But don't overdo it! Once in the greeting ("Hi [Guest]") and then once (maybe twice) more in the body of the mail is plenty. Any more than that and you risk coming across like a used car salesman!

7. PAY ATTENTION TO GUEST QUESTIONS.

Guests will inevitably ask questions. Sometimes many, sometimes just a few...but most of the time you will get the same questions over and over again. Instead of getting (understandably) annoyed at having to repeat yourself, use this opportunity to listen to and engage your guests. The last thing you want is to seem unfriendly or rude!

Another tip: answer some of the FAQs in the text of your property description (see Chapter 2). For example, if you *always* get a question like, "How far are you from the beach?" you should mention in your listing **at least twice** that you are "3 blocks to the beach" (or whatever). Unfortunately, this probably won't fix the problem completely, but it'll help.

Then, try to end your message with a question in return to keep the conversation going. Your guests will notice the extra attention, and might just choose your rental because of this small but important gesture.

When responding to inquiries, always be professional and polite...and **avoid grammatical errors**. This may sound rigid, but by being accurate and correct down to the grammatical details, you show guests that you take hosting seriously...and that they can trust they'll be in good hands with you.

AIRBNB CHECKLIST 03

HOW TO SCREEN POTENTIAL GUESTS

1. CHECK GUESTS' PROFILES
Verify IDs and learn about your guests
on their Airbnb profiles. Beware of
sparse info!

2. CHECK REVIEWS & REFERENCES
How have guests treated hosts before
you? Host reviews can give you an idea.

3. ASK TARGETED QUESTIONS
Messaging guests with the right questions
before a booking can tell you if they're a
good fit.

4. CONSULT SOCIAL MEDIA
Bare Airbnb profile? As a backup,
search their profiles on LinkedIn/
Twitter/etc.

5. RESPOND QUICKLY TO INQUIRIES
Good guests take their trip seriously
and value a fast reply. Keep them from
looking elsewhere!

6. USE THEIR FIRST NAME
Catch attention and create warmth
by using the guest's first name in
conversation.

7. PAY ATTENTION TO THEIR QUESTIONS
The questions guests ask can tell you
a lot about them. Be truthful and quick
with your response!

Chapter

04

CHECK-IN

WHEN STRANGERS BECOME FRIENDS

THE BIG MOMENT HAS ARRIVED. It's time to welcome your guests!

Don't forget to put yourself in their travel-weary shoes: likely they're dreaming of detaching from their luggage and crashing on your couch. The *last* thing they'll want is to be stranded on the street waiting for you. Especially if it's a freezing winter day in a land far, far away from home.

Establish a plan for a smooth check-in ahead of time. It's important, first of all, to be there the moment they arrive. Inevitably, your guests' plans will change at the last minute for all kinds of reasons. But if you have a backup plan, you can limit the pain for everyone.

Follow these tips to ensure a warm, personal and well-organized welcome for your guests!

1. COORDINATE CHECK-IN.

As mentioned above, a smooth check-in actually starts right after booking. Use the Airbnb messaging system to coordinate with your guests and **establish an arrival time.** This time can be fixed or flexible, as long as both parties communicate clearly and establish expectations (i.e., encourage them to text when they land, or when they're an hour away, etc.).

If your guests made their reservation a few months in advance, make sure to **send them a reminder a week before they arrive** with the pre-arranged check-in time.

2. WELCOME YOUR GUESTS IN PERSON.

You might be thinking: *Wait, I need to meet every group of guests at the property?* Call me old-fashioned, but yes! Other Airbnb hosts might hire management companies or leave keys with friends or neighbors, but there are so many advantages to meeting guests in person to kick off their trip.

First, the personal connection with guests is what Airbnb is all about. Don't cheat yourself out of that awesome moment when you discover you have something in common with a stranger from halfway around the world. Maybe you both have a special love for French bulldogs (or France). Maybe you have a mutual friend. Maybe you're both currently binge watching *Orange is the*

New Black. It reminds you how small the world really is!

Second, meeting your guests in person creates mutual trust. Your guests will be relieved to find that you are normal, friendly, and exactly who you said you were. And if all goes well, you'll feel the same about them. Also, importantly, when you meet your guest in person, they'll be compelled to **take better care of your house**. You'll be a real person to them...and someone they won't want to disappoint by leaving behind damage or a giant mess.

I know it's not realistic that you'll be there *every* time. (Or maybe I haven't convinced you!) In that case, by all means enlist a trustworthy friend or neighbor. Or put the key in a lockbox or a hidden place so guests can check-in themselves. Just make sure you give good instructions beforehand, and always have a spare key with a neighbor or friend in case your guests lose the key(s) and you aren't around to help.

3. ARRIVE 30 MINUTES EARLY.

Arrive at least 30 minutes before your guests to ensure your space is ready to welcome them. Open the windows to let in some fresh air. If you live in a hot area, turn on the air conditioning, or if it's very cold, get the heat cranking. Open the curtains and turn on the lights in living spaces, bedrooms and kitchen to create a welcoming ambiance.

4. PROVIDE A WELCOME GUIDE.

Airbnb provides the option to include a digital guide-book

for guests, where you can add recommendations for your favorite local restaurants and neighborhood activities. The personal touch is great, but the fact is, some travelers might want more than anything to get away from their computers/devices and disconnect.

Instead, **leave a printed Welcome Guide in an obvious spot** to share your tips, house rules and instructions. Also include emergency information, important details about your house, restaurant recommendations and other insider tips, and, importantly, your WiFi password ("disconnecting" doesn't count disconnecting from Netflix streaming!)

Keep the guide short. Once again, put yourself in the mindset of your guests: they are either exhausted, busy, or itching to get out and enjoy their vacation! Usually 2-4 pages is enough to cover everything.

5. GIVE YOUR GUESTS A TOUR.

After you welcome your guests, it's time to give them the grand tour. Take them through every room. Show them where to stow their belongings, what areas are off-limits (if any), and any special quirks about your place (that one window that sticks, the stray cat that hangs around the door in the morning, etc.). Explain the use of your electronics, appliances, and the heating and cooling systems. For the reasons mentioned above, your guests probably won't remember everything you said. That's when that hard copy Welcome Guide will come in handy!

6. FOLLOW UP THE NEXT DAY.

Once your guests are settled in, follow up the next day to see if they have any questions or concerns. This is a good time to solve any problems your guests are experiencing and prevent bad reviews at the outset.

7. COORDINATE CHECK-OUT.

You'll want to reach out to your guests one more time: the day before their scheduled check-out. It's the perfect moment to remind them of the check-out procedure and to say goodbye to your new friend! (More on this in Chapter 10.)

AIRBNB CHECKLIST 04

7 STEPS TO A SMOOTH CHECK-IN EXPERIENCE

1. COORDINATE CHECK-IN
Use Airbnb messaging to coordinate a check-in time that works for both of you.

☐

2. WELCOME YOUR GUESTS IN PERSON
Face time (and a "welcome" handshake) will create trust between you and your guests.

☐

3. ARRIVE 30 MINUTES EARLY
Prepare for your guests' arrival and make sure everything is clean, tidy and welcoming.

☐

4. PROVIDE A WELCOME GUIDE
Leave a printed welcome guide in an obvious spot to share your tips, house rules and instructions.

☐

5. GIVE YOUR GUESTS A TOUR
Take guests through each room and explain use of electronics, keys, heating/cooling, etc.

☐

6. FOLLOW UP THE NEXT DAY
Touch base to make sure their trip is off to a good start...and be ready to help as needed.

☐

7. COORDINATE CHECKOUT
Send a last message to remind them of checkout details (and to say goodbye to a new friend!)

☐

CLEAN YOUR CASTLE

DON'T TAKE IT LIGHTLY!

HAVE YOU EVER WONDERED ABOUT Airbnb's worst-case scenarios?

You know, those harrowing stories from hosts and guests that could almost scare you away from the idea of sharing a space with a stranger? Many of those stories have to do, in one way or another, with cleanliness. And cleaning. And contrary to popular belief, nightmare scenarios don't always have to do with messy *guests*.

Take it from me: it might actually be *worse* for a host when a guest cancels a reservation because he or she decides your house is filthy. It happened to me once...and it was a horrible experience. To my (pretty high) standards, the space was immaculate. But my brutally honest guest had an even *higher* cleanliness standard than mine, and found (and complained about) details I would have never noticed, like a subtle stain on the kitchen cabinets, a sticky light switch, and a stray hair on the bed.

At the time, I was a fairly new host, and I'd really tried my best to make the house welcoming for my guest. I was so disheartened by her complaints, and even more by the fact that she cut her stay short. The good part about this experience, though, was that I learned my two biggest lessons about cleaning for Airbnb guests.

LESSON 1:

Everyone's cleanliness standards are different. What seems clean to *you*...might not be clean to your guests. While you get your space ready, envision the pickiest, most detail-oriented guest you can imagine looking over your shoulder. If you clean for *them*, all your bases will be covered.

LESSON 2:

If you don't have the time or ability to give cleaning your full and careful attention, find a professional to do it for you. From the fateful day of that cancelled booking, I started my quest to find the best professional cleaners around. And I never looked back.

Over time, I've developed some shortcuts to make life easier for myself and the cleaners who help me. Whether you spring for professionals, or decide to do it yourself, these **Nine Cleaning Hacks** are essential for every Airbnb host to know.

1. STOCK BACK-UP SHEETS.

To make the turnover process simple, be sure to **have at least two sets of sheets and duvet covers on reserve**. It will save you a ton of time.

And definitely don't underestimate the time you (or your cleaning person) will spend doing laundry! It seems easy enough: throw a load in the washer; throw it in the dryer; done. But that's often not the case. Especially when you have multiple loads and only one washer and dryer...as is the case with most Airbnb hosts! A two-hour laundry job can quickly become a four-hour laundry job, which is a problem when you're dealing with a same day turnover.

Having enough clean sheets and duvet covers will make the whole process a breeze. No need to wait hours to start making the bed! Also, I recommend stocking cotton-poly blend sheets, which are ideal for quick turnovers (see Chapter 6). They're easy to launder, hardly wrinkle at all, and feel like 100% cotton.

2. WASH SHEETS AND TOWELS SEPARATELY.

It's tempting to throw sheets and towels into the same wash load. But towels shed lint on your freshly washed sheets, and lint is a time-consuming pain to remove (and remove them you must, unfortunately; remember, you're cleaning for those super-picky guests!). But you should buy towels and bathmats in the same color so *they* can be washed together.

When laundering your towels, skip the dryer sheets and fabric softener. They can leave a residue on the towels that makes them less absorbent.

3. DON'T FORGET THE KITCHEN CABINETS.

An often-overlooked spot is the exterior of the kitchen cabinets. (I learned this the hard way!) When it comes to kitchen cleaning, some jobs are obvious: the dishes get washed and put away, the stove is wiped clean and shiny. But the cabinets? It's easy to save those for another time.

In a rental, though, cabinets get dirty *fast*. Much faster than cabinets in a non-rental kitchen. Guests often leave greasy fingerprints, or splatter food while cooking their meals. Make sure you check them every time! (If you hire cleaners, of course, they'll *always* remember this step.)

4. LET YOUR DINNERWARE SHINE.

You'll find that many guests will wash their own dishes. Both out of kindness and because they know you're going to be reviewing them, too! But that's not a guarantee your dishes will be spotless. It goes back to that "cleaning standards" thing: your guests will wash the dishes to their standards, not yours...and not your pickiest guests' standards, either.

That's why, after your guests check out, you should check the dishes and glasses for sticky spots and stains... and double and triple check the flatware for smudges.

Spotless dishware, silverware, and glasses are a must for happy guests! No one wants to find fingerprints or lipstick stains right before their first bite or sip.

5. CLEAN MUCH-TOUCHED PLACES.

Remote controls, light switches, and doorknobs belong in the Top Ten list of dirtiest hot spots in the house, because they're also the most-touched places. Between every guest, **wipe down these hot spots** with disinfecting electronic-friendly wipes, even if they don't appear dirty. It's a quick, easy job, and it makes a big difference!

6. TAKE A VACUUM TO THE COUCH.

The couch is a centerpiece in your house, and it deserves special attention. Many bags of chips and bowls of popcorn will be enjoyed here. Use the upholstery brush attachment on your vacuum to get at stray hairs (and pesky pet hairs, too, if you have or allow pets).

Don't forget to lift those cushions! Imagine your guests searching for a cell phone that slipped between the cushions...only to discover the equivalent of a full meal under there! Not fun.

7. SAY HELLO TO YOUR NEW BEST FRIEND: THE LINT ROLLER.

Ever since the day my guest found a hair on the bed, the good ol' sticky lint roller has been my best companion.

After making the bed, **give your bed and sheets the once-over** to remove all hairs and loose lint. The lint roller also works great on the couch...use it as your final step to remove anything the vacuum cleaner left behind.

8. PROVIDE CLEANING PRODUCTS FOR GUESTS.

The last thing you want to do is give your guests a long list of chores to take care of in the midst of their vacation. Believe me, they won't appreciate it! However, you *can* encourage guests to clean up in more subtle ways.

For example, **keep cleaning supplies in plain view**. Like easy disinfecting wipes, microfiber cloths, multi-purpose cleaner, a mop and a vacuum cleaner. Even better, choose the good stuff: lovely-smelling, all-natural products that guests might not splurge on at home. I'm in love with the brands Method and Mrs. Meyer's Clean Day. The packaging is beautiful and their products smell so delightful...and on top of that, they're earth-friendly and non-toxic!

9. HIRE A PRO.

Feeling overwhelmed by all the above tips? Here's where I recommend (again) that you **outsource your cleaning to professionals.**

Cleaning for yourself is one thing, but cleaning for guests requires precise attention to detail and knowledge of how to clean specific areas very well. Most professional cleaners have years of experience and their standards of cleanliness are *industry* standards. In other words, they speak the same language as your pickiest guest!

Also important: they know which products are safe to use on each of the materials in your house (hardwoods, linens, tiles, marble, etc.). Plus, nothing beats the peace-of-mind you get from finding reliable cleaners you can really count on, even when you're out of town.

HOW TO FIND A GREAT CLEANER

I've talked with many Airbnb hosts, and we've all had good experiences posting ads on Craigslist or just asking around among friends and other hosts (if you don't know hosts in your area, try an online Airbnb group).

Though I hesitate to recommend it, you *can* also book a cleaner through cleaning startups, which matches you with a network of professional cleaners in your area. In other words, it's like Uber for cleaning services. And, like Uber, booking through these companies is quick and easy.

But be warned! That convenience could come at a cost.

Because these services operate on a nationwide scale, the risk is high. I asked other Airbnb hosts about their experiences with large cleaning startups, and the comments were far from positive. Horror stories include cleaners not showing up, not being able to find the keys to enter the house, and general scheduling issues. And when you have guests arriving in mere hours, you have to be 100% sure that the room is going to get clean on time... and cleaned well.

Worse, since bookings can be very irregular, you might not get the same cleaner every time...which leads to having to review your specific cleaning procedure every time a new cleaner arrives.

Again, though they are convenient, I would *not* recommend using any large cleaning startup for your Airbnb rental.

The best thing I did in my Airbnb hosting career was **hire a reliable, local cleaning crew recommended to me by another host.** Because they're a team, they do the job faster and better than an individual. Each person focuses on a specific area, so they can be thorough and quick.

Keep in mind, I'm emphasizing the importance of cleaning for one important reason: **your reviews**. You want those golden 5 star-reviews! (Airbnb research shows listings with 5-star reviews receive 20% more inquiries). Also, take it from me: getting a cancellation on the first day of someone's stay is an uncomfortable situation you'll want to avoid.

If you do decide to clean the rental yourself, turn to the "Resources for Accidental Hosts" section at the end of this book. I've included a cleaning checklist to help you prep your space like a pro!

AIRBNB CHECKLIST 05

9 AIRBNB CLEANING HACKS

1. STOCK BACK-UP SHEETS
A stack of fresh, clean sheets makes the
turnover process much smoother.

2. WASH SHEETS AND TOWELS SEPERATELY
Towels shed lint on your freshly washed
sheets...and they're a pain to remove!

3. DON'T FORGET THE KITCHEN CABINETS
Most guests will open the cabinets at least
once. Sweep out crumbs and wipe down doors.

4. LET YOUR DINNERWARE SHINE
Make your dinner and flatware investment
gleam. No fingerprints or lipstick stains
allowed!

5. CLEAN MUCH-TOUCHED PLACES
Doorknobs, light switches and remote
controls are the dirtiest hot spots.

6. TAKE A VACCUUM TO THE COUCH
After the bed(s) are fresh, treat your rental's
other centerpiece: the sofa. Lift those cushions!

7. A LINT ROLLER: YOUR NEW BEST FRIEND
Hairs are guests' worst nightmare! Give
sheets and pillows the once-over to remove
clingers.

8. PROVIDE GUESTS CLEANING PRODUCTS
Many guests will pitch in during their stay if
you leave an all-purpose cleaner in plain sight.

9. HIRE A PROFESSIONAL
Not sure you have the time to commit to
spotlessness? Hire a cleaner! You won't regret it.

THE DETAILS

THE BEDROOM

PREPARE A PERFECT SLEEP SPACE

IT'S AN UNWRITTEN LAW OF travel: after a long day in a plane, train, or car (or--horrors!--all three) we all long for a warm welcome...and a fluffy pillow. Many of your guests will come in, drop their bags, and faceplant directly on the bed for a minute (or an hour).

That's why paying attention to your guest bedroom is one of the most important things you can do to create that "this is going to be a great trip" feeling for your guests the moment they arrive.

When I just started hosting on Airbnb, I was mostly concerned about the basics: a comfortable bed, clean sheets, and a stack of clean towels. It was only after a few years of hosting that I learned the secrets to creating a room that guests really don't want to leave. And it all had to do with delighting the five human senses.

We'll start with the obvious: **nothing is more inviting than a beautifully made bed**. It's the centerpiece of a bedroom, so make it stand out! Splurge on a thick duvet and fluffy pillows. The more cloud-like, the better. Not only do these touches make the bed *look* inviting, they welcome your exhausted guests with a downy embrace that will have them sighing with happiness.

Other details do great work, too: a soft rug warms up the room and provides a soft landing for feet in the mornings; a beautiful throw blanket at the foot of the bed delights the eye; freshly cut flowers give a room a natural fresh scent; and splashes of color throughout can have a huge impact on a person's mood. Who knew that a subtle touch of red could spark a little romance?

Remember: a bedroom is not just a place to sleep. Your guests will use the bedroom to recharge after a busy day, withdraw from the conversations in the living room, catch up on work, read a book, have some quiet time, and yes... get romantic. If you have to choose *one* place to transform into a sanctuary, choose the guest room. Your guests will thank you for it!

1. CREATE A HEAVENLY BED.

Some people love their own bed so much they wish they could bring it with them when they travel! As a caring host, you want your guests to sleep as if they were at home (or even *better* than they do at home).

But it can be a challenge to meet the sleeping needs of so many different guests. A comfortable mattress is key, of course, but let's be realistic: a high-quality mattress is expensive.

Luckily, there's a way to upgrade your old mattress without having to spend a lot of money right away: **add a down feather bed on top of your mattress**. (I stole this brilliant trick from vacation rental expert Alanna Schroeder of The Distinguished Guest!). A featherbed adds a fluffy layer to your mattress and costs between $75 - $200--significantly less than a new mattress.

When it *is* time to replace your mattress, buy one with a medium-firm surface. It will work for almost every sleep preference. Also, be sure to protect your feather bed (or mattress) from spills and stains with a *waterproof mattress protector*. As for the size of the bed: opt for at least a queen mattress. A full-sized one might be too small for couples.

2. INDULGE WITH DOWN & FEATHER PILLOWS.

There's nothing worse than an old, stained, lumpy pillow. On the other end of the spectrum, though, is a true bed-time indulgence: a down-and-feather pillow. Not synthetic. Down and feather pillows are softer and can be easily shaped for your guests' optimal comfort, while synthetic fill doesn't contour well and can develop lumps. Hypoallergenic or memory foam pillows are also a great choice if you'd rather not use down (and your allergy-prone guests will love you, too)!

As with your mattress, **cover your pillows with a pillow protector** to prolong their lifespan and keep them clean. Bonus: pillow protectors are much easier to launder than the pillows themselves. Simply take it off and throw it in the laundry with your bed linens!

3. LAYER CRISP WHITE SHEETS.

Who says you can't give your guests a hotel-like experience in your home?

I know, I know...Airbnb is all about staying in authentic places, or even *anti*-hotel places, but when it comes to bedding, nothing beats the white crisp sheets you'll find in most hotels.

Many vacation rental experts I've talked to agree on this: great-quality sheets are a difference maker. Though you might hear a lot of people recommend 100% cotton sheets (and for good reason), **don't overlook good, quality cotton/polyester blend sheets**. They're super-easy to launder, wrinkle-resistant and feel very soft and comfortable.

Plus, they look amazing from the moment you pull them out of the dryer! This makes the cotton/poly blend perfect for busy Airbnb rental hosts and cleaning staff who have precious little time between guests but still want the place to look sharp.

Important: As covered in Chapter 5, make sure to have *at least* one extra sheet set and duvet cover to make the turnover process much smoother.

Then, finish the look with some color: subtle splashes

of red in a nice decorative pillow or throw blanket have been known to induce a little romance. (Yes, your guests will have sex in your guest bed! And, in truth, you want them to, because it means they're enjoying themselves. Might as well help the process along!)

Check out Etsy for some cute and unique throw pillows and blankets. They're a nice alternative to those same four or five IKEA pillows that you spot at countless rentals across the world! (Note: I love IKEA. But when it comes to throw pillows, you can do better!).

4. ADD CONVENIENCE WITH BEDSIDE TABLES.

Two small nightstands are a must-have in every guest bedroom. Here is where your guests will keep important items like books, eyeglasses, reading lights, and yes, their smartphones. Make sure there's plenty of space for all of it!

In addition to being a very useful piece of furniture, nightstands are the perfect bedroom accessories, too. They create symmetry, and symmetry creates a feeling of balance and calm.

5. DON'T FORGET THE READING LIGHTS.

Pay attention to the lighting in your bedroom. Reading lamps on each nightstand bookending the bed are not only necessary for guests who love to read before falling asleep, they also give the room a cozy ambiance and are within arms reach when your guests need to get up in the middle of the night.

6. WARM THE ROOM WITH A SOFT RUG.

One of my favorite items to add to a bedroom is a soft area rug. It will immediately add color, warmth, and coziness to your room--not to mention a soft landing for your guests' feet first thing in the morning! Place a small rug on each side of the bed to optimize that feeling. You can also place a large rug under your bed. Just make sure it's large enough to encompass both sides of the bed.

7. GIVE GUESTS A DESK NOOK.

Adding a desk to your room is great for the business travelers you may host. And even those on a relaxing vacation might find themselves using it to write something down, plan their travel itineraries, or catch up on emails. It can also double as a vanity table for putting on makeup!

The desk is also a great, visible spot to place a guestbook. Here, guests can leave you a thank you note or make recommendations for your next guests. It's a nice touch that shows off one of the many ways Airbnb rentals are different--and more personal--than hotels!

8. PROVIDE A COMFY ARMCHAIR.

If you have the space, consider a comfortable chair. An often-overlooked addition, a chair is a great spot for putting on shoes, reading a book, or unwinding after a long city walk. Guests won't always want to come home and immediately curl up in bed, after all! A comfy chair is a nice transition spot.

9. CLEAR ROOM IN THE CLOSET.

Make ample closet space for your guests so they can hang their clothes and store their belongings. It let your guests know they're welcome! Opt for chic cedar hangers to make your closet look sophisticated.

AIRBNB CHECKLIST 06
9 GUEST ROOM ESSENTIALS

1. UPGRADE YOUR BED WITH A FEATHER BED □
A featherbed on top of your mattress gives heavenly comfort to grateful guests.

2. CHOOSE DOWN & FEATHER PILLOWS □
Two down pillows per guest is the ideal set-up for a luxury sleep.

3. CREATE A HOTEL VIBE WITH CRISP SHEETS □
Buy the best cotton or poly-cotton blend sheets you can afford—it's worth it!

4. ADD CONVENIENCE WITH BEDSIDE TABLES □
A table at each bedside keeps books, eyeglasses, water, and coffees in reach.

5. DON'T FORGET THE READING LIGHTS □
Reading lamps or lights are a must for bedtime reading and cozy ambiance.

6. WARM UP THE ROOM WITH A SOFT RUG □
Usher guests gently out of bed with a plush rug for warm and cozy feet.

7. GIVE GUESTS A DESK NOOK □
Guests love a tidy desk space for work catch-up or adding to the guestbook.

8. PROVIDE A COMFY ARMCHAIR □
What beats a quiet corner space to read or unwind after a full day of travel?

9. CLEAR ROOM IN THE CLOSET □
Ample closet space with cedar hangers lets your guests know they're welcome.

Chapter 07

THE BATHROOM

GUESTS ARE COMING...HIDE THE PILLS!

EVERY ROOM IN YOUR HOUSE needs to be fresh and clean when you're hosting guests...but, as you'd imagine, the bathroom in particular needs to be polished to perfection.

And if you plan to share a bathroom with your guests, you'll need to do some extra preparation. Declutter the bathroom, empty a drawer for your guests, and remove anything you'd rather not share. Don't overlook the medicine cabinet! Most of us have items in our medicine cabinets that are...well, *personal.* (In other words, hide the pills!)

Also, you want your guests to be comfortable in your bathroom. That means providing everything they need to solve any "just-in-case" bathroom incidents. You *really* don't want guests to remember their stay as "that time they clogged the toilet and..." You get my point. So provide a plunger, citrus spray, and plenty of toilet paper!

Here are some other bathroom must-haves:

1. CLASSIC BATH TOWELS.

Becoming an Airbnb host is a *great* excuse to **buy new, good-quality towels**. Old, faded, musty towels just won't cut it anymore! Donate your old towels to an animal shelter...or repurpose them into cleaning cloths. Then, go get yourself some new, soft, classic bath towels your guests will love!

The towels don't have to be expensive to be good-quality. Mercedes Brennan, a hospitality interior designer specializing in vacation rentals, says that her favorite towel also happens to be the cheapest: the FRÄJEN towel from IKEA. In fact, I've heard more than one person declare their love for IKEA's towels.

Now, if you have a high-end listing, with a $1000-a-night rate, it makes sense to get luxurious towels. In all other cases, though, go for the middle ground; towels are on the list of products you'll need to replace on a regular basis.

Look for **durable towels that are medium-thick**. Super-thick towels, nice as they are, take up a lot of space in the washer and take forever to dry. And as I've stressed throughout this book, you want the turnover/laundry process to be as speedy and stress-free as possible!

I recommended cotton-polyester blend bedsheets in Chapter 5, and the same applies to towels. Cotton-poly towels will make laundering a breeze. As for the color?

White is the classic hospitality choice because it conveys cleanliness and matches everything.

Be warned, though: white can be high-maintenance. Every stain is clearly visible...and that bright whiteness doesn't last forever. You'll likely need to replace them more often than towels in other colors. So, if you're more practical, choose colors like light grey, beige or a shade to match your bedroom linens. Buy the set so that your towels, hand towels and washcloths all match each other, too.

Wash and dry your new towels before putting them out for guests. But as I mentioned in Chapter 5, don't use fabric softener or dryer sheets. Both can leave a waxy film on your towels that can make them less absorbent.

2. CABANA/BEACH/POOL TOWELS.

If you live near the beach, or if you have a pool, don't forget to include a separate set of towels. Most likely your guests won't bring their own beach/pool towels, and they'll be relieved you thought of it. **This is important:** do *not* give them that faded, perpetually chlorine-smelling beach towel from 10 summers ago! It doesn't matter if your guests pay $500 a night or $50 a night, they deserve a little luxury.

Look for cabana towels instead. The gorgeous white with blue stripes adds a resort-style touch to your rental--perfect for lounging poolside or at the beach on a sunny day. You don't have to pay a boatload, either! I bought mine at **The Distinguished Guest**--a great online store for beautiful vacation rental amenities and linens.

3. A THIRSTY BATH MAT.

Bath mats are the most overlooked bathroom must-have. I hardly ever hear people talk about them! Even Airbnb cleaning services talk about providing "towels and clean sheets"...and I always wonder, what about the bathmat?

No one wants to put their feet on a dirty mat (or worse, a dirty bare floor!) after a shower.

You know I'm all about streamlining my cleaning, and I've found some great tips when it comes to your bathmat operations. (Yes, seriously! I've put a lot of thought into this!)

First, as we covered in Chapter 5, for practical reasons you should **choose a mat in the same color as your towels**, so you can wash and dry it all together. Also try to find one *without* rubber on the bottom of the mat; they can't be put in the dryer at all.

My favorite bath math is the TOFTBO Bathmat by IKEA (see, I told you I love IKEA!). It's made from microfiber and feels incredibly soft on your feet. What I love most about this bathmat, though, is that it just keeps looking great. I've used other, more expensive mats that don't stay as nice as this one...which costs just $9.99. On top of that, the TOFTBO can be thrown in the dryer and it comes in a wide range of colors to match your bath decor.

If your bathroom is small, you can also fold the TOFTBO, which will make an even softer landing! Like I said: it's my *favorite* mat, and really, the only mat you'll ever need.

4. A HAIRDRYER.

Your guests will be grateful the moment they find a hairdryer in your bathroom. Many will have reluctantly left theirs at home to save precious suitcase space...and basically, they'll feel like they've left behind their right arm. In fact, some might even book your place based on the fact that you have a hairdryer! Trust me, it's not as crazy as it sounds. It's a small investment and it pays off.

Really want to impress your guests? Present it in a beautiful pouch.

5. PERSONAL CARE PRODUCTS.

Want to really set yourself apart? Provide your guests with toiletries. This will save them from that frazzled trip to the drug store for a forgotten item, and they'll love you for it.

I've spent a lot of time weighing the options for what size and type of personal care products to provide. Here's my take:

FAMILY-SIZE AMENITIES: THE PRACTICAL, EARTH-FRIENDLY OPTION.

The most practical, earth-friendly options (with the least waste) are giant, family-size pump style bottles, like Pantène shampoo and conditioner. I've stayed at several Airbnb rentals that provided these in the shower, and I immediately filed this extra touch into my "hosting tips and tricks" database. It's cheap, easy, thoughtful, and won't send a ton of tiny bottles into the landfill.

Be sure to check between guests to make sure the bottles have plenty of product left. And don't forget to refill your hand soap pump with delicious-smelling liquid hand soap every time, too! (More on this in Chapter 7.)

TRAVEL-SIZED AMENITIES: THE PRETTY, WOW-YOUR-GUESTS OPTION.

Can I make a confession, though? The large bottles, as environmentally friendly and convenient as they are, don't always *look* as nice as luxury guest toiletries. If you really want to spoil your guests, go ahead and provide travel-sized luxury bath amenities, brand-new for every guest. The option lends a hotel/resort feel to your bathroom: clean, fresh, and pretty.

It can be surprisingly difficult to get good small bars of soap and small bottles of shampoo in beautiful packaging for a reasonable price. Drugstore versions are usually expensive (and don't look nice!). Thankfully, I discovered two online retailers that I love: BNB Goodies and The Distinguished Guest. BNB Goodies sells luxury guest toiletries for a very reasonable price, and they have three lines to choose from to capture the style and spirit of your house. The Distinguished Guest offers not only high-quality bath amenity kits, but also spa slippers and general amenities (toothpaste, toothbrush, mouthwash, personal care kits and more) to give your guest a 5-star experience. Check them out!

6. A PRISTINE SHOWER CURTAIN.

If you use a shower curtain, mildew build-up is pretty

much inevitable (and nasty!). Regularly check the curtain and liner for mildew and soap scum, and make sure to launder it in the washing machine when needed. To make it easier, take a cue from hotels and, instead of vinyl shower curtains, use ones made from polyester or nylon. They're a breeze to wash. Check Bed, Bath and Beyond for their line of shower curtains called "Hotel." They're even mildew resistant!

7. BATHROOM EMERGENCY KIT.

Now we come full circle in this chapter...back to bathroom emergencies. Remember: using someone else's bathroom is uncomfortable enough. And it's worse if you become the protagonist in a bathroom "incident." Toilet clogged and no plunger, not enough toilet paper, no trashcan... this is all the stuff of nightmares. Have mercy on guests and provide all of these, plus citrus spray and matches to neutralize odor.

Emergency supplies for the ladies will be appreciated, too (nail files, bobby pins, etc.).

AIRBNB CHECKLIST 07

7 BATHROOM ESSENTIALS

1. CLASSIC WHITE BATH TOWELS
White towels convey clean. Choose medium-thick over super-thick—they're easier to launder!

2. CABANA BEACH OR POOL TOWELS
Have a pool, hot tub or beach close by? Striped cabana towels have a high-end resort feel.

3. A THIRSTY BATHMAT
My all-time favourite is the $10 TOFTBO microfiber bathmat at IKEA. You're welcome!

4. A HAIRDRYER
Give guests the gift of luggage space! Keep a hairdryer in a pretty pouch for chic convenience.

5. PERSONAL CARE PRODUCTS
Provide shampoo, soap and other care products. Bonus points if they're earth-friendly!

6. A PRISTINE SHOWER CURTAIN
Regularly check the shower curtain and liner for mildew and soap scum between guests.

7. BATHROOM EMERGENCY KIT
Create a bathroom basket with citrus spray/matches, first-aid items and extra goodies.

Chapter 08

THE KITCHEN

"ALL HAPPINESS DEPENDS ON A LEISURELY BREAKFAST." - JOHN GUNTHER

I DON'T KNOW ABOUT YOU, but the most memorable moments from my travels always involve food.

My earliest vacation memories take me back to the Belgian Ardennes, where my family would spend summer vacations picking and eating blackberries during long mountain hikes. Little did I know it would only get better as I got older! A few years later, during a vacation in France, I lost my food virginity in a French restaurant eating escargots in garlic butter, fried frog legs, lemon meringue pie and crème brûlée...all in one truly incredible, unforgettable meal!

In their "real lives" your guests are hurriedly squeezing meals into their days. Even those who love to cook sometimes have no choice but to grab an energy bar for the morning commute instead of breakfast, or to hit up the dreaded drive-thru for dinner.

But here, on vacation, they can take their time to cook and eat and really enjoy food. To prepare their favorite dish. To enjoy a long and leisurely breakfast with the company of people they love. To share a romantic dinner accompanied by a splurge bottle of wine.

That's why it's so important to have kitchen essentials that allow guests to make the most of their culinary time. I'm talking about **sharp knives, cutting boards for meat and cheese, and large pots for pasta.** And then comes all those small items that you only remember when you *don't* have them, like a corkscrew for wine or beer.

I'll detail some of these kitchen must-haves below!

A note: When you pick items for the kitchen, **make low-maintenance a priority**. You want products that can survive sharp knives, the dishwasher, or hours of soaking in water. You *don't* want to worry about your favorite cutting board being used or cleaned inappropriately and getting damaged... and your guests shouldn't have to either!

1. A GOOD, SHARP KNIFE.

No need to buy a full knife block. You'll spend most of your chopping/peeling time with the same two or three knives: a versatile Chef's knife to cut through dense/large vegetables or meat, a small vegetable knife for tasks like peeling apples and slicing garlic clove, and a bread knife for freshly baked bread (also great for slicing tender fruits).

That's it!

2. DISHWASHER-SAFE CUTTING BOARD.

As much as I love wooden or bamboo cutting boards, they will get cracked and ruined in the dishwasher. Which, in my book, makes them a rental kitchen no-no, unfortunately. You can warn your guests not to put them in the dishwasher, but chances are, *someone* is going to forget sometime.

Instead, go for dishwasher-safe. One less thing to worry about! A decent option? Epicurean cutting boards. They're dishwasher-safe, very durable and made from natural wood fiber material that can mimic the rustic look of a wood cutting board.

3. NON-STICK FRY PANS.

When it comes to convenient cooking, **a quality non-stick, dishwasher-safe pan** is the way to go.

Do keep this in mind, though: most nonstick pans are made from Teflon, which at very high temperatures can release toxic fumes and chemicals. Many of your guests will have heard about this, and have perhaps already transitioned to a different kind of fry pan in their own kitchens.

That's why you should **look instead for one of the "green" or "healthy cookware" options**, which are non-stick *and* free of these chemicals. Specifically, you want non-stick pans that are labeled PFOA and PTFE-free. Greenpan is a great choice, and affordable at only about $19.95.

What about the trusty **cast iron pan**? I know some

people swear by it! The downside of cast iron, though, is that it must be seasoned frequently and shouldn't go in the dishwasher. In the end, it's a pretty high-maintenance piece of kitchen equipment for a vacation rental. So, unless you are dedicated to taking care of it regularly, I don't recommend it. With maybe one exception: to impress your gourmet-inclined guests, you can provide a *small* cast iron pan in addition to the non-stick pans.

4. SHINY STAINLESS STEEL POTS.

Provide a stack of **dishwasher-safe, stainless steel pans**, too. These low-maintenance pans look great and stay gleaming after many uses! Just check the label to make sure they're *actually* dishwasher safe.

Another tip: hang your pots and pans on the wall for a stylish look. A nice, elegant set begs to be showcased! This also makes it easier for your guest to find the right pan (no need to dig around in your cupboards).

5. WORKHORSE KETTLE & COFFEEMAKER.

Remember what I said about breakfast? Your guests are going to want to relish in a long, slow morning, where they can sip coffee or tea without jetting off to their next obligation. Don't forget to keep your rental stocked for these moments! **Coffee, sugar and cream are a must.**

Also have some earl grey and herbal tea, and provide a kettle, too. Both electrical kettles and the whistling, stove-top kind work just fine. However, they do have some key differences. The stove-top kettle is nice to look at, and all but your most kitchen-averse guests will know how to use them. Electrical kettles might intimidate some guests, but they heat water faster and have an automatic shut-off valve that's engaged once the water starts to boil. This feature is a lifesaver (literally, in some cases) if your guests are forgetful and walk away from boiling water.

As for coffee, I love the French press. It makes a solid cup of coffee; it's easy to use; and it has more longevity than an electric coffeemaker. Drip coffee (like a Chemex) is a great alternative, as well.

6. HEAVEN-SCENT DISH SOAP.

Provide dish soap with nice scent for your guests. Not only does it save them from that lingering, old-sponge smell on their hands (yuck!), it might wordlessly encourage them to do the dishes.

Buy a large refill bottle of the soap you choose and make sure to top it off between every group of guests. I really like the brand Method for its smell and look. And I'm *obsessed* with the basil-scented soap from Mrs. Meyer's Clean Day. Both brands are earth-friendly and non-toxic, too!

7. MATCHING DINNERWARE.

Up the sophistication factor at your rental with matching dinnerware. It doesn't have to be expensive...and, actually, it *shouldn't* be expensive. After all, dinnerware is subject to chips, cracks, and fractures, and it shouldn't be a dramatic event if a guest accidentally breaks a plate. This applies even if you have a high-end rental. The important thing is that it looks chic!

Buy dinnerware that's easy to find, so if (or more realistically, *when*) a guest breaks a glass or plate, you can replace it in a second. Let's go back to our old friend, IKEA: they keep the same dinnerware in their stores for a long time, so replacement is never a hassle. Other dishware lines (like those found at department stores) might be discontinued after a season or two, so beware.

Once again, you'll want to go for microwave and dishwasher-safe. The most versatile choice is plain white dinnerware. It's inexpensive, easily replaceable, and won't fade with every dishwasher cycle.

8. FANCY FLATWARE.

Here's where I think you can (and should!) go fancy: the flatware! Eating with gleaming, sculpted, nicely designed silverware seems to make the food taste better, doesn't it? Unlike glasses and plates, silverware won't easily sustain damage, so it's much safer to spend a little extra.

9. WOODEN SPATULAS.

To protect your pots and pans, stock your kitchen with wooden spoons and nylon spatulas instead of metal. If possible, present them in a countertop utensils holder, like flowers in a vase, so guests don't have to rummage through the drawers.

10. A SALAD BOWL

Bring out the beauty of well-dressed greens with a large salad bowl. As much as I love wooden salad bowls, I can't quite recommend them as, once again, they aren't dishwasher safe (boo!). Opt for glass or stainless steel instead.

Unless, that is, you don't even *have* a dishwasher. In that case, go for wooden. (This same tip applies, by the way, to cutting boards. If you don't have a dishwasher into which your guests can put your not-dishwasher-safe items, then by all means, buy wood and bamboo! Though you will have to accept the risk that your guests won't want to bother with hand-washing, and instead leave stuff in the sink for you to take care of.)

11. PRETTY KITCHEN TOWELS

Nothing brightens your kitchen like colorful towels. Don't forget to mix it up with different patterns and colors! Unlike in the bathroom, matchy-matchy towels in the kitchen are...well, pretty boring. The queen of seductive cooking, Nigella Lawson, agrees with me: "A kitchen should never look decorated: it's just needs to feel lived in." (Don't we all have a crush on Nigella?)

Swapping out kitchen towels is like an instant makeover. If your kitchen is beige, avoid beige towels. Opt instead for a color that pops, or maybe some old-fashioned, square-printed towels.

You'll need to provide at least two kitchen towels (one for hands, one for dishes) and wash new towels before putting them out for guests.

12. CAN OPENER.

A few important things to know about this handy tool:

First, it, too, should be dishwasher safe. Second, it should be rustproof. And third, it shouldn't come in contact with the food (for hygienic reasons). Yes, these requirements do add up to a more expensive can opener, but see it as another opportunity to wow your guests with an unexpected indulgence.

I've done some research for you. Try the Rosle Stainless Steel Can Opener!

13. BOTTLE & WINE OPENER.

Don't let your guests face the frustration of a full bottle of wine and no way to get to it! Choose a classic winged corkscrew for its multifunctionality.

14. PASTA STRAINER.

Understandably, guests like to make pasta during their vacation. It's such an easy and versatile dish. Plus, the strainer is quite handy for washing those leafy greens we're all supposed to be eating daily!

Bonus: Leave basics like salt, pepper, and oils in the pantry. Your guests will only need to use a fraction of each, and making them buy the full-size versions on their grocery store trip is a bit cruel, isn't it?

AIRBNB CHECKLIST 08

KITCHEN ESSENTIALS FOR YOUR AIRBNB RENTAL

1. A GOOD, SHARP KNIFE
Skip the knife block. A quality Chef's knife, vegetable knife and bread knife are all you need.

☐

2. WOOD CUTTING BOARD
Wood-grain cutting boards are durable, rustic, and can double as cheese & snack platters!

☐

3. NON-STICK FRY PANS
For safety and convenience, choose dishwasher-safe, non-stick pans free of PFOA and PTFE.

☐

4. SHINY STAINLESS STEEL POTS
A polished set of stainless steel pots are great to cook with and look good hung on the wall.

☐

5. WORKHORSE KETTLE & COFFEEMAKER
Caffeinate guests for years with a sturdy coffeemaker and kettle. Consider these an investment!

☐

6. HEAVEN-SCENT DISH SOAP
Attractively packaged, fragrant dish soap and a new sponge will persuade guests to clean up.

☐

7. MATCHING DINNERWARE
Mind your guests' mealtimes with chic, matching dinnerware. It shows you care about details!

☐

AIRBNB CHECKLIST 08 contd.

KITCHEN ESSENTIALS FOR YOUR AIRBNB RENTAL

8. FANCY FLATWARE
Delightful dishes need well-designed, matching flatware. The good stuff has heft to it.

9. WOODEN SPATULAS
Wooden spoons and spatulas protect your pans. Bonus: they have a nice farmhouse look.

10. A SALAD BOWL
Bring out the beauty of well-dressed greens!

11. KITCHEN TOWELS
Nothing brightens your kitchen like colourful towels. Swap them out for an instant makeover.

12. CAN OPENER
A great handheld can opener is dishwasher safe, rustproof and opens bottles, too (see below).

13. BOTTLE & WINE OPENER
Don't let your guests face the frustration of a full bottle of wine and no way to get to it!

14. PASTA STRAINER
If your guests are after a quick, easy meal to make on vacation, pasta will top their list.

THE LIVING ROOM

KEEP IT COZY!

THE LIVING AREA IS A shared space. A place where your guests will have conversations, watch movies, eat snacks, and take rejuvenating naps.

In this room, interior design is going to play a very important role. The colors of the wall, the artwork you choose, the furniture you bring in...all of these will influence your guests' mood and enjoyment of the space. Your aim is for them to feel relaxed, calm, and inspired. In short, your living room should be a place they'll be happy to return to after a day of exploring.

The good news? Creating that feeling doesn't take an interior designer's budget!

1. AVOID TONS OF PERSONAL MEMORABILIA.

New hosts often ask me whether they should remove all their personal items and photos from their home before they rent it out.

The best advice I've heard so far on the topic comes from staging expert Meredith Bayer: there's a difference between showing *personality* in design and filling a space with *personal items*. Too many pictures of you and your friends/family and your guests will feel like trespassers!

Instead, decorate with *personality*. Incorporate pieces that reflect your personal style, including original art and even, yes, a well-placed artistic photo that has you in it. One of my clients, for example, hung a gorgeous, artistic photo of her and her beloved French bulldog Pippin in her hallway. It was the perfect balance: guests got a sense of her as an owner and person, but since it was in the hallway, they were not confronted with it at every turn.

2. ILLUMINATE YOUR LIVING AREA.

More than any other factor in your living room, light will directly affect the way your guests feel. Research shows that when humans are deprived of light, they become depressed. And I don't know about you, but for me, a dark room in mid-day feels deeply oppressive. It makes me want to flee immediately!

If your house has lots of **natural light**, lucky you! You're halfway there already. If it doesn't, avoid decorating with oranges, reds, browns and blacks, as they will absorb all the light. Go for white or pale shades of green, blue, and lilac--colors that will amplify and reflect the light.

As for electric lights, your focus should be on **accent lights,** including table lamps and candles. Overhead lights are helpful when guests want to find their way around your house, but they don't contribute to a relaxing and cozy atmosphere.

If you have a couple of reading nooks, place a good light next to the seating area for book lovers.

3. SPEAK TO YOUR GUESTS WITH BLUE.

Did you know that blue is the most-liked color worldwide? It's been shown to have a calming effect. Which also happens to be *exactly* how you want to make your guests feel. Decorate in shades of blue and your guests from every corner of the world will love it!

Be leery of decorating with an abundance of earthy tones like browns and beiges. These can make your space feel dull and uninspiring. **Mix it up!**

4. CREATE CONVERSATION AREAS.

Make it easy for people to talk to each other. Scoot the seating a little closer. For a casual vibe, sprinkle a few floor cushions for people who like to sit low.

5. GET ARTFUL.

Do you have an eye-catching artwork in your home?

A beautiful designer lamp or an original painting you cherish? An exposed brick wall or a mid-century sofa? Make this the centerpiece of your room. *And* make sure that it's visible in your listing photos. Today's guests love to be surrounded (and inspired) by beautiful things!

6. GO BIG OR GO... SHOPPING.

My Dad used to tell me not to buy large furniture for my room; it'll only make the space look smaller. When I was a teenager, I believed everything he said. But now I know better, and this is one of the times he was flat-out wrong. Large items actually make your space look *bigger.* A large rug, for example, draws the eye outward and expands the space.

7. MIX, MATCH, MISMATCH.

Don't be afraid to mix patterns and different materials. I used to try to match everything--bed, bedside tables, closet--but now I see and appreciate eclectic, surprising combinations that look fantastic together. Some great mix-and-match combos include a metal bed paired with modern wood side tables, and a leather sofa with a wool or faux fur throw. And don't be afraid to put a bold color on a piece of furniture. All of these make the room look more interesting and increases your "bookability"!

8. MAKE IT SOFT & COZY.

Warm up the room with high-quality decorative pillows,

a nice throw blanket on the couch, and a large, soft rug. The best tip I've heard about pillows, from interior designer Mercedes Brennan, is to *not* cheap out on them. Spend time picking good ones. Good-quality pillows can upgrade a so-so couch, but cheap pillows will cheapen even the nicest one.

After hearing this tip, I looked at my couch with another eye. My pillows were anything but uplifting. I decided to go shopping for new ones, and it made a huge, immediate difference.

As I mentioned in Chapter 6 for the guest bedroom, keep an eye on Etsy. They have a great collection of original, handmade pillows and throw blankets!

9. HOUSEPLANTS: NOT JUST FOR GREENTHUMBS.

I'm the last person in the world to give advice on plants. Even cacti die on me! But I haven't given up yet. I love nature and I sometimes feel as we've lost touch with it, so I'm happy that houseplants have made a comeback. In response, I'm slowly starting to include and care for plants in my house. They really liven the space!

If, like me, you don't have green fingers, fear not. There are easy-to-maintain options like succulents and aloe vera plants, which prefer dry soil and very little watering. A range of cacti on a nice copper plate or a fiddle leaf plant in a corner will make any living room look amazing.

Great with plants? By all means, fill your place with plants that make you happy! They'll make your guests happy, too.

AIRBNB CHECKLIST 09
8 TIPS FOR A COZY LIVING ROOM

1. AVOID TONS OF PERSONAL MEMORABILIA
Too many personal items and guests will feel like trespassers! Show them your home is theirs.

2. ILLUMINATE YOUR LIVING AREA
Nothing helps ambiance like light. Open blinds, add lamps and decorate in a soft color palette.

3. SPEAK TO YOUR GUESTS WITH BLUE
It's the most popular color worldwide! Bring a touch of blue to your décor to calm and attract.

4. CREATE CONVERSATION AREAS
Scoot seating closer together or into an L shape. Floor pillows are also great for gathering around.

5. GO BIG OR GO...SHOPPING
Don't let the room swallow your furniture! Give everyone a place to sit on a big, comfy couch.

6. MIX, MATCH & MISMATCH
Go ahead and mix colors, patterns and fabrics. Opposites attract in decorating, too!

7. MAKE IT SOFT & COZY
Think back to piling in for a sleepover. Add lots of throw pillows and downy-soft blankets.

8. HOUSEPLANTS: NOT JUST FOR GREEN THUMBS
They're not *all* finicky. Hardy plants like cacti bring your room to life with little effort.

CHECK-OUT

BID ADIEU TO YOUR NEW FRIENDS!

HERE'S HOW YOU'LL KNOW YOU'VE reached Accidental Airbnb Host nirvana: when your guests say they'll be back. Or that they'll recommend your place to friends and family. Once you have bid adieu to your first happy, glowing, well-rested guests, you're not an accidental host anymore. You're a true hospitality professional.

The compliments from guests make all the hard work worth it! But beyond the ego boost, if you're planning to make this into a true, year-round vacation rental business (as opposed to a side gig when you're traveling or need some extra cash), you have to start thinking long-term strategy. You *want* guests that will come back year after year.

And you can achieve that by exceeding their expectations right up to the last moment of their trip. Here's how to make the "farewell" as good as the "welcome."

1. PREPARE GUESTS FOR CHECKOUT.

A day or two before your guests are set to leave, send them a friendly reminder of your checkout procedure. Also consider arranging a time to meet up before they take off. This is especially important if they have stayed in your home *with* you and you've spent some time getting to know each other.

Want to take a step further and *really* send them off with great feelings about their trip? **Give them a small parting gift** like a box of homemade cookies, a bottle of local olive oil, or another small souvenir. You may win a friend (and a customer) for life! And beyond the potential repeat bookings/5-star reviews/recommendations, these small but much-appreciated gestures can make both parties feel warm and fuzzy about the overall Airbnb experience.

Of course, it's entirely possible your guests will be rushing around to catch flights, trains, etc., so if your "goodbye" plan doesn't pan out, don't stress. Guests can do the checkout procedure themselves. And really, it's the thought that counts. They'll appreciate that you cared enough to *want* to see them off, even if it doesn't work out.

2. PUT THE GUESTBOOK IN PLAIN SIGHT.

Ask your guest to leave a note in your guestbook, with suggestions for future guests, comments, or memories they'd like to share. If you're a great host, you'll find your guests will use the guestbook to thank you and gush about their good experience. (See my note above about the Airbnb warm fuzzies!)

Be sure to leave the guestbook open in an obvious spot. They'll be more likely to contribute!

3. DO A POST-GUEST CHECK.

Do a quick post-guest check to make sure everything is in good shape, undamaged, and functioning as it should.

If you have added a security deposit to the nightly rate, you have 48 hours from your guest's checkout date to make a claim before it is automatically released back to them. Hopefully you won't need to keep the security deposit due to guest-inflicted damage, but if you do, make your claim at www.airbnb.com/resolutions.

If your guests agree to the amount, Airbnb will process the payment and send you a payout. If you don't hear back from your guest within 48 hours, you can choose to let Airbnb to mediate by clicking "Involve Airbnb" in your Resolution Center case.

It sounds intimidating, and it's good to be prepared, but fear not! Most guests are just like you and me: normal, friendly people who will try their best to treat your home with respect.

4. REVIEW YOUR GUESTS ASAP.

Both you and your guest will have 14 days to complete your

reviews of each other. Don't wait until your guest writes their review before writing yours. It may never happen! Instead, go ahead and write first; it'll trigger them to give feedback, too. Both of you will only be able to see the review if you *both* leave one, so the incentive is high for both host and guests. Also, when you write the review, you have the option to leave a personal, private note. Use it! Include a line that welcomes them back should they visit your area again.

5. BE HELPFUL AND HONEST IN YOUR REVIEW.

Keep in mind that Airbnb is a global community of hosts and travelers. Other hosts will thank you for your honest reviews of guests. There are two main things other hosts will want to know: **how did the guests treat your house**, and **how well did they communicate?**

If you had some issues with your guests that were resolved during their stay, you don't necessarily have to mention this in the public review. But you can mention it in a *private* message if someone asks. Use your common sense. If you feel there are things about the guest that other hosts should know, mention it in the public review, but be polite: start with mentioning the things you liked about your guests. Then mention the things you didn't like, and frame it in a constructive (not mean or snarky) way.

6. PAY ATTENTION TO GUEST REVIEWS.

Since we're not all hospitality experts from the start, it's important to take guest reviews seriously. They help you find out what your guests loved about your place and what they didn't...including things you hadn't thought about before. I remember back in my early days of hosting, a guest review mentioned that I should decorate the room more and include facecloths in the bathroom. Though I would consider these essentials *now*, back then I clearly wasn't aware of their importance. Information like this is gold: it will help you improve your listing with each guest stay.

7. STAY IN TOUCH FOR REPEAT BOOKINGS.

If you and your guests really bonded, keep in occasional contact through email and social media. They'll think of you the next time they're in town! I've friended guests from Argentina on Facebook, for example, and the next time I go to Buenos Aires, they are the first people I'll call for a drink.

AIRBNB CHECKLIST 10

7 STEPS FOR A SMOOTH CHECKOUT

1. PREPARE GUESTS FOR CHECKOUT
A reminder of checkout procedures,
sent 1-2 days beforehand, will keep the
steps fresh.

2. PUT THE GUESTBOOK IN PLAIN SIGHT
Leave the guestbook open in an obvious
spot, with a pen. They'll be more likely to
contribute!

3. DO A POST-GUEST CHECK
Test to make sure everything is functioning
at 100%. Try water faucets, electronics,
locks, etc.

4. REVIEW YOUR GUESTS ASAP
Reviewing will trigger your guests to give
feedback, too!

5. BE HELPFUL IN YOUR REVIEW
Hosts will thank you for honest info. How
did the guests treat your house? Did they
communicate?

6. PAY ATTENTION TO GUEST REVIEWS
Listening to feedback will help you improve
your listing after each guest stay.

7. STAY IN TOUCH FOR REPEAT BOOKINGS
Keep in occasional contact through
email and social media so they'll think
of you next time!

AFTERWORD

ACCIDENTAL HOSTS, I HAVE ONE more piece of advice for you.

In my experience, there's a time *before* hosting on Airbnb and a time *after*.

In the time *after*, I started to see the world a little more optimistically. I was continually surprised by the goodness and generosity of people I didn't know a day (or even an hour) ago. Do bad experiences happen on Airbnb? Of course. But most strangers you meet will be truly lovely people with something to teach you about their slice of the world.

There's another shift that happens after you start hosting, too. If you're like me, you will go from "accidental host" into "I should have started this months ago!" host.

Then, as the great reviews start rolling in, you'll start to host more guests more often.

At that point, what once seemed like a one-time thing quickly turns into a serious business.

But my advice? Don't lose sight of the *fun* part. Like all successful business owners, you have to love what you do...at least most of the time. If you don't have fun, it's likely your guests won't either. That's why I've stressed throughout this book the importance of streamlining your operations. Using products that are easily replaceable, resistant to damage, and guest-friendly at the same time are essential to keeping you sane and your guests happy.

As more and more people join the Airbnb community (and with a community this open-minded, well-traveled, and people-focused, who could blame them?!), it becomes even more essential that your Airbnb listing rise above the crowd. I hope the tips and tricks that I shared in this book will help create your own 5-star haven!

And, even though this book sometimes reads like one big list of DOs and DON'Ts, feel free to make your own rules--just as long as those rules benefit both you *and* the guest. Don't forget (there I go again!) that it's the unique blend of *you* as a person and *your* one-of-a-kind sanctuary that guests will appreciate, and what makes Airbnb and vacation rentals the new face of hospitality.

ACKNOWLEDGEMENT

FIRST AND FOREMOST, I WANT to thank Kevin Darmody, founder of Urban Bellhop, for introducing me to the world of hospitality and for helping me bring my hospitality skills to the next level. It was exciting to be a part of one of the first service providers for Airbnb hosts!

I'm beyond grateful for having met fabulous vacation rental professionals during my time at Urban Bellhop. Thanks to Mercedes Brennan at OneChicRetreat for opening my eyes to the importance of interior design for vacation rentals (and avoiding stinky kitchen sponges).

Thanks to Henry at BNB Goodies for teaching me how to keep hospitality simple, even in high-end listings. Thanks to Alanna Schroeder from The Distinguished Guest for your support, and for being a wonderful curator of vacation rental amenities I can count on. Your collection of products not only are the best guest treats, they make my life easier!

The year spent writing this book was a true indulgence, not only because I got to hole up and spend hours and hours in coffee shops writing, drinking coffee, and just blissfully staring off into space, but also because I was able to work with amazingly talented people. Thank you to my talented friend Latorri Lindsay for making the artwork for this book. You have to know that I'm your number one fan. I'm so happy that I got to work with Carolyn Brown from Ten Deer Sigh, who designed the interiors of my book so beautifully.

I still can't get over my luck in having worked with Jessica Vozel from Guest Hook, who edited this book. Without her I would definitely have had "bookshame"--I would not have put this book out into the public with confidence if it wasn't for her.

I want to thank my husband, Melvin, for making this book project possible and for your endless love and support. A special gratitude for my friends and family for allowing me to share little pieces of the book with them. A big thank you for the amazing hosts who trusted me with their homes and guests. And lastly, I give a heartfelt thanks to the wonderful guests from around the world that I got to meet throughout the years, especially the picky ones - you challenged me to become a better host each time.

ABOUT THE AUTHOR

VERONICA TERCAN GOT HER START at Urban Bellhop, helping Airbnb hosts create and market their rentals and facilitating hundreds of bookings. Before that, she spent two years as an Airbnb host herself, welcoming guests from all around the world to her San Francisco apartment. Originally from The Netherlands, Veronica currently lives in the Bay area with her husband and cat.

CONTACT AND ADDITIONAL INFORMATION

I HOPE YOU ENJOYED THIS BOOK! For more tips and tricks on how to create a 5-star vacation rental, visit: www.theaccidentalhost.com. While there, you can sign up for my newsletter to receive regular updates and great free content.

To download or print my Airbnb checklists, you can find them at: www.theaccidentalhost.com/checklists.

For questions or just to say hello, please write me at: veronica@theaccidentalhost.com.

Extras

RESOURCES FOR
ACCIDENTAL HOSTS

THE GO-TO AIRBNB CLEANING CHECKLIST

BATHROOM

- Wipe all surfaces
- Wash and disinfect toilet, shower, tub & sink
- Clean door handles & light switches
- Wipe mirrors & glass fixtures (don't leave streaks!)
- Vacuum & mop floors
- Take out trash & recycling
- Stock toilet paper
- Change towels
- Clean inside medicine cabinet
- Replace towels & bath mat
- Refill hand soap dispenser
- Replace/refill toiletries
- Check hair dryer
- Replace toilet paper roll

KITCHEN

- Wipe all surfaces
- Clean stove, counter tops, oven & fridge exterior
- Wipe exterior of cabinets & other appliances exteriors
- Clean sink & unload dishes
- Clean interior & exterior of microwave

- Vacuum & mop floors
- Take out trash & recycling, replace bags
- Check glasses & plates for stains & fingerprints
- Check utensils & cutlery trays for cleanliness
- Wipe inside fridge
- Refill dish soap
- Wash or replace sponge
- Clean water filter & coffee maker
- Replace kitchen towels

BEDROOM AND LIVING ROOM

- Replace sheets, duvet cover, pillowcases
- Go over sheets & pillows with lint roller
- Dust and wipe all surfaces
- Clean door handles & light switches
- Vacuum & mop floors
- Check under bed
- Clean remote controls
- Vacuum couch & go over with lint roller

EXTRA

- Wash sheets separately from towels
- Provide deliciously scented cleaning products for your guests
- Stock extra sheets & duvet cover

KITCHEN ESSENTIALS FOR YOUR AIRBNB RENTAL

FLATWARE

KNIVES

CUTTING BOARD

KITCHEN CLOTH

PLATES & GLASSES

SALAD BOWL

WOODEN SPATULA

STEEL POTS

SOAP DISH & SPONGE

STEEL PANS

CAN OPENER

BOTTLE OPENER

PASTA STRAINER

COFFEE MAKER

VERONICA'S TESTED TOOLS

PROFESSIONAL PHOTOGRAPHY

The most important thing you can do to catch your guests' attention and increase bookings is to hire a professional to take photos of your rental. Request a professional photographer on Airbnb for free at https://www.airbnb.com/info/photography.

WRITING YOUR LISTING DESCRIPTION

Having trouble writing the property description of your vacation rental? Hire professional travel copywriter Jessica Vozel of Guest Hook. Jessica has helped countless property owners boost their bookings with sharp, targeted property descriptions. And she's a gem to work with, too! Request more information at www.jessicavozel.com.

INTERIOR DESIGN TIPS

Mercedes Brennan is the Queen of vacation rental interior design. Her popular blog will help you decorate your way to more bookings! She also offers a range of interior design services, from consults to full home redesigns. Sign up for her newsletter at www.onechicretreat.com for amazing decorating tips.

VACATION RENTAL AMENITIES

Want to give your rental a resort feel? Look no further than Alanna Schroeder at The Distinguished Guest. Alanna traveled the country to find the best hotel-quality sheets, luxury amenity kits, and more for vacation rentals, all at a great price! Purchase these products at www.thedistinguishedguest.com.

COTTON-POLY BLEND SHEETS

Cotton-poly blend sheets are a dream for busy Airbnb rental hosts (and cleaning staff) who want a sharp place but have precious little time between guests. Cotton-poly is super-easy to launder, wrinkle-resistant and feels soft and comfortable. Check out the crisp 60/40 blend sheets with pima cotton at www.thedistinguishedguest.com.

HYPO ALLERGENIC PILLOWS

A true bedtime indulgence is a down-and-feather pillow. Hypoallergenic or memory foam pillows are also a great choice. Worried about down allergies? The Distinguished Guest has pillows that are *both* down-and-feather pillows *and* hypoallergenic, too. www.thedistinguishedguest.com.

BATH TOWELS

To make the turnover/laundry process as speedy and stress-free as possible, I recommend durable, medium-thick towels, like the FRÄJEN from IKEA. They stay looking like-new for a long time, and are easily replaceable. Another great choice is cotton-poly towels, which will make laundering a breeze. Also available at www.thedistinguishedguest.com.

CABANA/POOL/BEACH TOWELS

The gorgeous white with blue stripes adds a resort-style touch to your rental. I bought mine at The Distinguished Guest. www.thedistinguishedguest.com.

BATH MAT

So you finally got to meet my favorite bathmat: The TOFTBO bathmat by IKEA. This baby is soft on the feet and looks great after hundreds of post-shower drips. Plus, the TOFTBO can be thrown in the dryer *and* it comes in a wide range of colors to match your bath decor. Only $9.99 at IKEA. www.ikea.com.

PERSONAL CARE PRODUCTS

The most practical, earth-friendly option (with the least waste) are giant, family-size pump style bottles. Be sure to check between guests to make sure the bottles are clean and have plenty of product left. Want to go for luxury amenities with an earth-friendly and organic touch? Find them at www.thedistinguished.com and www.bnbgoodies.com.

PROFESSIONAL CLEANERS

Find local and trusted cleaning professional! Many Airbnb hosts have had good experiences posting ads on Craigslist or just asking friends and other hosts (if you don't know hosts in your area, post your question in Airbnb's community center). https://community.airbnb.com, www.craigslist.com.

DISHWASHER SAFE CUTTING BOARD

Epicurean cutting boards are dishwasher-safe, very durable and made from natural wood fiber material that can mimic the rustic look of a wood cutting board. www.epicurean.com.

NON-STICK FRY PAN

When it comes to convenient cooking, a quality non-stick, dishwasher-safe pan is the way to go. Look for one of the "green" or "healthy cookware" options. Specifically, you want non-stick pans that are labeled PFOA and PTFE-free. Greenpan is a great choice, and affordable at only about $19.95. www.greenpan.com.

DISH & HAND SOAP

Choose lovely-smelling, all-natural products that guests might not splurge on at home. I'm in love with Method and Mrs. Meyers Clean Day. The packaging is beautiful and their products smell so delightful...and on top of that, they're earth-friendly and non-toxic! www.mrsmeyers.com, www.methodhome.com.

DINNERWARE

Buy dinnerware that's easy to find, so if (or more realistically, *when*) a guest breaks a glass or plate, you can replace it in a second. IKEA keeps the same dinnerware in their stores for a long time, so replacement is never a hassle.

DECORATIVE THROWS & PILLOWS

Check out Etsy for some cute and unique throw pillows and blankets. They're a nice alternative to those same four or five IKEA pillows that you spot at countless rentals across the world! www.etsy.com.

NOTES